Right Start for School

JEAN ANDERSON
SUSAN FISCHGRUND
MARY LOBASCHER

Longman

LONGMAN GROUP UK LIMITED
Longman House
Burnt Mill, Harlow, Essex CM20 2JE, England
and Associated Companies throughout the World

First published 1989
ISBN 0 582 04433 2

Set in Scantext 11pt on 12pt Syntax

Printed and bound in Great Britain by
Courier International Ltd, Tiptree, Essex

Contents

Foreword   4
Introduction   5

MOTOR SKILLS AND MOVEMENT   7

Large movement skills   8
Fine movement skills   19
Pre-handwriting skills   28
Visual skills   34
Drawing people   38

SPEECH AND LANGUAGE SKILLS   43

Body parts   44
Personal information   46
Position and direction words   49
The alphabet   52
Colours   57
Talking and conversation   58
Reading to your child   59
Memory words   64
Stimulating imagination   67
Number   70

SOCIAL SKILLS   73
Dressing   74
Eating   75
Toiletting   76
Sharing   77
Respecting property at
school and at home   77
Learning to take turns   78
Lending and borrowing   78
Planning and organisational skills   78

Foreword

Right Start for School has been written to help parents prepare their child for going to school. It lists the skills a child should have learnt before starting school and suggests how parents can help their child to become confident in using these basic skills. Settling into school is difficult for some children but children who are secure in these physical and social skills will find this new experience less frightening and even enjoyable!

Parents want their children to have the best possible start in life but they may need advice and suggestions – not instructions – on how to prepare their child for the next hurdle to be jumped. To have to spend several hours a day with many other children of their own age, and without their parents, is quite a hurdle.

The authors give their advice clearly, with sensitivity, and even a sense of humour. They write with confidence but without that dogma that can make advice on how to bring up children so irritating.

They avoid giving the age when a certain skill should be learnt because they know that no two children are the same. They also know that no two mothers or fathers are alike and that the parents' personalities will inevitably and rightly influence the ways they handle their children. There are no 'perfect parents' and if they existed they would, I suspect, make a bad job of bringing up their children!

As a paediatrician who has tried to help older children still suffering from the unhappy experiences of their early school days, I welcome *Right Start for School.* It successfully fills a gap in educational literature.

Professor Otto H. Wolff C.B.E., M.D., F.R.C.P.
Emeritus Professor of Child Health
University of London

Introduction

Going to school is probably one of the most important experiences of a child's life. It requires new disciplines for learning, paying attention and contributing. For some children it may be the first prolonged contact with others of the same age, and this experience can produce both pleasure and pain. Memories of successes and failures may last a lifetime and the effects of a bad beginning can take years to overcome.

Children spend much more time at home than they do at school. As a parent you have been, and still are, your child's most important teacher. There is so much you can do with your child at home to make his school experience more meaningful.

This book helps parents and children discover success and enjoyment earlier and to avoid failure and disappointment later. It is hoped that by offering your child these opportunities to establish early learning skills his first school days will be rewarding and enriching.

The 'right start' activities, the first learning skills in this book, were chosen because we as educationalists have found that they form a package of essential abilities especially related to good adjustment and success in early, and then later, school life. Parents may draw on the activities suggested in the book to suit their child's individual needs and to build his confidence in his own ability. It cannot be too strongly emphasised how important it is for positive attitudes to be established and achievement to be experienced during the child's first year at school.

> NOTHING SUCCEEDS LIKE SUCCESS!

Whilst it is hoped that parents and children will enjoy the activities in Right Start, it must never be forgotten that a child's spontaneous play is as important as any formal teaching. Play is life-enhancing, encouraging creativity and self-direction, both vital to a child's well-being.

Right Start is divided into three sections:

1 Motor skills and movement
2 Speech and language skills
3 Social skills

Although shown separately, these areas of development all interrelate and it can be seen from some of the suggested activities how two or more skills are used together.
    Each activity will show:

● The skill to be taught
● Why it is necessary to learn the skill
● How to teach the skill
● How to improve and practise the skill through activities and games
● Related benefits of the skill, i.e., transfer effects which improve other skills.

Please remember that the *stages* of development are the same in all children and it is only the *rate* of development that differs from one child to another. For example, a child generally crawls before it stands, stands before it walks, and walks before it runs; but some children walk at eleven months and others at eighteen months. Some children talk at fifteen months and others at two and half years. These rates all fall within the normal range of development. In all cases it is possible to promote and strengthen the development of these skills.
    The *Right Start* programme uses objects commonly found in the home but you may wish also to purchase some of the items referred to in the book.
    'Right Start' skills should be practised in as relaxed an environment as possible, and only for as long as your child enjoys the task. Never start games if you are in a hurry, feeling low or if your child is tired or unwilling.

AIM HIGH, START RIGHT, HAVE FUN!

Motor is a term used to refer to movement, both large and fine, and to the position of the body (posture).

Motor skills are divided into:

Large movements The child's ability to use his whole body in a well co-ordinated way.

Fine movements Those abilities which enable the child to make appropriate small physical judgements and carry out well co-ordinated hand/eye movements.

Body image The awareness of the parts of the body, the knowledge of left and right, directions such as down, up, across, over, etc., and positions such as in, on, above, in relation to the child's own body.

You will find some ideas for learning body image words in the language chapter. Here, suggestions are given to help your child improve the use of his body in a practical way.

Large movement skills

Why?

Large movement skills are essential for an individual's full development. The mastery of these skills will help your child to become better co-ordinated, independent and self-assured. Vigorous physical activities stimulate body processes, thus encouraging better sleeping and eating habits. The child with inefficient motor skills is apt to withdraw from people around him, which may then result in social problems with his companions. If co-ordinated large movement skills are not established early in a child's development, it is more difficult for him to achieve them in later years.

The most common skills your child should acquire in his early years are:

● Balancing
● Running
● Hopping
● Skipping
● Jumping
● Catching
● Throwing

Balancing

Balancing is necessary for the safe performance of many physical tasks presented by a child's environment.

How to teach balancing

Remember that balancing should be performed with controlled, deliberate movements, rather than with fast jerky ones. Get your child to progress through the following exercises:

- Stand on one foot briefly
- Stand on the other foot briefly
- Stand on one foot for several seconds – stand on the the other foot for several seconds. Increase time according to your child's ability.
- Hold your child's hand while he is standing on one foot. If several children are around, form a circle and hold hands while they take turns in standing on one foot.

Practice activities and games

If your child is having difficulties with balancing, these activities may help.

Let your child look at pictures of people and animals and imitate their stances.

Examples:

"Can you stand on one foot like the bird in this picture?"
"Can you stand like the man leaning over the gate?"

When tying your child's shoe, ask him to lift his foot up whilst holding on to you for support.
Ask your child to balance on his preferred leg with arms outstretched to the side, and time him in seconds with a watch or stop-watch. Gradually increase the time on a reward system using sweets or stickers, or raisins etc.

Lay string, rope or tape across the floor. Ask your child to walk on it heel to toe.

Let your child stand on one leg, arms to the side, then direct him to move his arms to specified positions whilst he remains standing on one leg.

Examples:

"Put your hands on your hips."
"Put your arms above your head."

Repeat the activity, with your child using the other leg. Let him support himself against a wall to start with.

Knee lifts and stork stands Ask your child to stand with his arms out, whilst you hold his waist. He then lifts one knee until the thigh is parallel to the ground. He should hold the position for a few seconds before returning to a standing position. Repeat the exercise, using the other leg.

Tell your child to put all his weight on one foot and place the sole of the other foot against the calf of the standing leg. Ask him to hold that position for a second or two and then return to standing position.

It may be more fun for your child if you do these exercises together, taking it in turns to choose what to do with your hands or arms.

Simon says Practise the game 'Simon says'. For example: "Simon says balance on one leg, put up one arm". This can be amusing if music is used to stop and start the action.

Other activities Using string, tape or rope, form a figure eight on the ground and ask your child to walk or run on it.

Ask him to try spinning like a top and remaining upright!

Walking, running, skipping and hopping are all skills related to balancing.

Running

How to teach running

Outdoors Begin in an outdoor area. Ask your child to run once around the field, garden, or play area.

Small objects Let him practise running with a small object, such as a soft toy to a target such as a bucket, basket or

cardboard box. He should place the toy in the box and return to the starting point.

Egg and spoon races Let your child run whilst carrying an item such as a small potato in a spoon.

Animal movements Ask him to run whilst imitating various animal movements, for example, horses, elephants, mice, cats, etc.

Obstacle course Arrange an obstacle course with furniture, boxes, toys, etc., and ask your child to run the course; or arrange a maze and ask him to find his way out of it without crossing the barriers.

Zig-zags Ask your child to zig-zag round four or five objects placed on the ground in the garden or park.

The ability to run in a co-ordinated way can be greatly improved with practice. Through playing some or all of the above games frequently he will have fun whilst improving running skills.

Hopping

How to teach hopping

- Stand in front of your child
- Ask your child to stand on his preferred foot
- Whilst holding both of his hands, ask him to take a little jump forward on that foot, without letting the other one touch the ground

- Progress to holding one hand and letting him try two or three jumps
- Change to the other foot and repeat the exercise

Ask your child to try to hop independently on his preferred foot. Progress to getting him to hop across an area of three feet.

Skipping

How to teach skipping

Skipping requires precise rhythm, timing and balance, so it is essential first to practise the balancing and running skills already discussed.

Hold your child's hand and move slowly through the movement pattern,

- step
- hop on the same foot
- other foot forward (to the ground) and hop
- repeat, using the other foot.

When your child knows the pattern of skipping, increase speed to get a fluid movement.

When possible, children enjoy skipping to music.

Jumping

How to teach jumping

- Place a small soft object, for example a bean bag, small soft toy or hat, between your child's ankles or knees.
- Whilst he holds the object in position, ask him to try to jump on the spot without dropping it.
- Progress to getting him to make small forward jumps on a flat surface.
- Then, progress to jumping backwards or jumping off a low surface such as a step.

Hopping, skipping and jumping practice activities and games

Hop-scotch There are many variations of this game but, basically, the player is required to throw a counter or small stone into one of the squares and to hop from one square to another to reach the square with the counter in it.

Snake jump On a flat surface, place a long rope, or hose-pipe over which the child can jump zig-zag fashion.

Cradle swing Two players gently swing a rope close to the ground from side to side. The child jumps over it until he is 'out' or 'over'. Gradually raise the height of the rope.

Mind the lines When out walking, let your child practise running, hopping or jumping between the lines of the paving stones.

Catching

How to teach catching

● Start with soft, lightweight objects, for example, bean bags, fluffy balls, soft toys.

● Initially show your child how to catch the object by using his arms and his body in a hugging manner. Let your child sit on the floor to 'catch' a ball rolled towards him.
● Your child can then use his arms and body to catch a bounced ball.

- Slowly encourage your child to use his arms only, and to catch away from his body.
- Progress to standing and catching a ball thrown gently underarm.
- Progress to catching with both hands only.

Throwing

How to teach throwing

- Begin by letting your child roll a ball on the ground.
- Progress to throwing lightweight objects, using both hands.
- Then encourage him to use his preferred hand to throw, using first the underarm and then overarm action.

Catching and throwing practice activities and games

Pass the ball Hand the ball to and fro between you and your child. If there is more than one child in the family, extend the activity, sometimes using music to stop and start, as in 'Pass the parcel'.

Containers Practise throwing a ball into a container, such as a grocery box, waste-paper basket or bowl.

Targets Practise throwing a ball or soft item to hit a specific target such as an empty can or plastic bottle.

Bouncing Show your child how to bounce a ball, beginning with a large ball and progressing to smaller ones.

Other games Most children's ball games are of benefit for developing ball skills.

Examples:
Tunnel ball
Throwing a ball through a hoop, etc.
Rolling a ball along a garden path.

Helpful suggestions

Some children have difficulty in following spoken directions and will profit from a demonstration by either you or another child. Demonstrate *one step at a time*, allowing your child to copy each step in turn.

   Your physical assistance helps. Actually move your child's body through the exercise so that he gets the *feeling* of what he needs to do before he starts the action on his own. Use any opportunity which arises to practise the skills discussed.

Repetition develops the strength, co-ordination and endurance required for complex, physical skills; which most of these activities represent for a young child.

Using the suggested guidelines, be inventive with materials and games to retain your child's interest.

Benefits of good motor co-ordination

- Physical independence
- Good judgement of space
- Increased hand/eye skills
- Better sporting ability
- Active participation in group games
- More energy
- Increased confidence

Fine movement skills

Fine, precise movements are required for many of the skills we perform throughout our lives. More particularly they are an essential pre-requisite for writing and self-help skills, such as dressing and eating.

Fine movement skills refer to:

Fine motor co-ordination This is the ability to carry out by hand and eye small, fine movements, for example: cutting, buttoning, threading, pasting, etc.

Motor perceptual skills This is the child's understanding and judgement of how he relates to objects in space around him. Educationally these skills affect his ability to copy shapes and patterns and therefore to write.

Motor co-ordination

How to teach fine movement skills

Always progress from large to small movements. When developing fine movement skills, begin with large objects that are easy for a child to handle. As the small muscles of your child's hands and fingers become efficient introduce smaller objects.

Allow plenty of time for free play. Give your child many opportunities to play with the materials being used.

Create a varied environment in which your child should be given activities that involve drawing, colouring, painting, finger painting, tearing large pieces of paper, modelling with plasticine or play dough, cutting and pasting, paper weaving, buttoning, lacing, zipping, opening and closing doors and latches, etc.

Practice activities

Building with blocks

Materials
Coloured blocks

Procedure
Start with a limited number of blocks and later increase the number.

Allow time for your child to build freely with the blocks.

Discuss the different shapes and colours of the blocks.

Use a few blocks to make a simple pattern for your child to copy.

Talk about the pattern as you put the blocks in place.

When your child can copy your pattern, let him make a pattern for you to copy.

Let him try copying a pattern from memory!

Pegboards

Materials
A peg board and a set of coloured pegs (easily obtainable from toy shops).

Procedure
Give your child an opportunity to experiment with pegs and peg boards by himself.

Using the peg board, make a pattern for your child to copy.

Always talk about the pattern as you put the pegs in place. For example "I am putting in 1 green peg, 1 red peg, 1 yellow peg", or "I am putting in 2 greens, 2 reds, and 1 yellow".

Let your child copy your pattern. Encourage him to tell you what he is doing as he copies your pattern. *His talking will improve his thinking skills.*

When he is able to copy your pattern correctly, ask him to make a pattern for you to copy.

Let him copy a pattern of colour combinations from a drawing.

Ask him to look at a pegboard pattern then remove the pattern. Let him try to copy·the pattern from memory.

Puzzles

Materials
Jig-saw puzzles, 'fit-in' toys, 'posting' toys, and toys with colourful, easily handled parts.

Procedure
Begin with puzzles that have large, thick pieces. Later, let your child use puzzles that have thinner, smaller pieces.

When using jig-saw puzzles, *always* show a completed puzzle to your child before he begins.

Discuss the picture in *great* detail.

Scatter the pieces again and let your child try to put the puzzle together.

Offer as much help as necessary in the beginning, for example, advice about straight sides, corners, and matching colours.

Clothes peg drop

Materials
Household containers such as cardboard boxes, jars with different size openings, and a set of clothes pegs, paper clips or stones.

Procedure
Tell your child to stand upright immediately in front of a container.

He should hold the peg waist-high, above the container.

He must drop the peg directly into the container.

Progress to using containers with smaller openings.

Stringing objects

Materials
Beads, curtain rings, buttons, straws cut into pieces, macaroni bits, pipe cleaners, shoe laces, string or thread.

Procedure
Start with thicker threads, such as pipe-cleaners and large objects, such as curtain rings.

As co-ordination improves, progress to thinner threaders and more complicated objects.

Ask your child to copy the pattern you thread, using coloured beads.

Allow him to make his own pattern from a variety of objects, e.g., milk bottle tops, pasta pieces, buttons.

Pouring

Materials
A large bowl of water, jugs and cups.

Procedure
Arm your child with an old plastic jug and mug.

For as long as it amuses him, allow him to fill the jug with water from the bowl or bath, pour it into the mug, empty the mug and begin again.

This is preferably an outdoor activity, alternatively, a bath-time one!

When sufficient progress has been made, allow your child to practise pouring juice or milk into his own cup.

His growing independence is well worth the occasional spill.

Cutting with scissors

This is a most important school readiness skill which we feel should be carefully taught. It develops fine motor skills and visual judgement. The ability to cut with scissors brings satisfaction and pleasure to a young child, especially in art projects, and is a practical skill for use throughout his life. The following suggestions will help you to teach your child this skill.

At first, use paper that is easier for a beginner to cut (that is, greeting card weight).

Keep a box of old Christmas cards, birthday cards, wrapping paper and magazines.

Provide good quality scissors, blunt tipped and about twelve cm (five inches) long. Left-hand scissors should be provided for left-handed children.

Have empathy! In order to experience how difficult and frustrating cutting can be for the beginner, *you* try cutting a piece of cloth with the hand you do not usually use.

Show your child how to hold a pair of scissors, that is, using thumb and forefinger in a clasping movement.

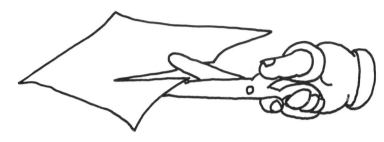

Allow plenty of time for your child to practise the 'cutting movement' in the air, without the scissors. Let him pretend he is 'cutting' air.

Introduce him to scissors and paper. At first, hold the paper for him so that he can concentrate on the cutting.

When he can cut paper without help, teach him to turn the paper, not the scissors, when changing direction.

When he gets better at cutting, thinner paper, e.g., magazine weight, may be used.

Safety rules Your child should be taught:

- to keep the scissors away from his face
- to carry the scissors closed and with the tips down
- to hand the scissors from one person to another handles first
- *never* to put scissors into pockets!

Correct teaching sequence for cutting

Place thumb and fingers in handles of scissors and grasp scissors correctly.

Practise the cutting motion with the scissors by moving the thumb and fingers against each other.

Cut into a piece of paper, using one scissor stroke at a time. This may be repeated along the edge of the paper.

Allow time for free cutting. i.e., no lines to follow.

Progress to cutting between two drawn lines – three cm (one inch) apart.

Cut a piece of paper, staying between two lines one cm
   (a quarter of an inch) apart.
Cut along a straight line.
Cut along a wavy line.
Cut around a circular line.
Cut into and out of wide angles.
Cut into and out of smaller angles.

Some fun ideas

Make your own scrap-book Cut out attractive, colourful,
pictures from magazines or cards, and paste them into a
large blank page scrap-book. Allow your child to do as
much of each task by himself as he comfortably can.

Make a collage Let your child cut out coloured paper,
cards, scraps of fabric, etc., Let him experience cutting
and handling materials of different textures, e.g., tweed,
silk, macaroni, leaves. Let him help as much as he is able
to make the collage.

Draw simple shapes Draw crosses, circles and squares, for
your child to cut out and paste into his scrap-book. Let
him attempt to draw, cut and paste his own shapes.

Cards Encourage your child to design and make simple
greeting and Christmas cards. A child's original work is
greatly appreciated by family and friends.

27

Pre-handwriting skills

Handwriting requires controlled pencil movements, an awareness of direction and size, and your child's ability to use his eyes, moving from left to right. All these skills can be helped prior to starting school by using some or all of the following activities.

Left to right eye movements

It cannot be emphasised enough how important it is to encourage the habit of left to right eye movement as a pre-reading and pre-writing skill.

Practice – here's how!

Help your child become familiar with the 'feel' of books. Emphasise turning pages from left to right. Discuss how the story unfolds, always from left to right and, when reading stories, encourage him to turn pages in the correct order. Allow him to look through a book from beginning to end, following the story without skipping pages and by looking at the pictures.

Picture stories such as comic-strips and picture books, will encourage your child to discover independently how story sequences move from left to right.

Count in sequence using bottle tops, blocks, toys, buttons or stones to count from 1 to 10. Place in a row or rows,

and moving from left to right, teach your child to count one object at a time. Move from row to row and, using a finger to touch each object, again ensure that he touches each item as he counts it. This reinforces correct eye movement as well as accuracy in counting.

Use several rows of objects to illustrate how to move from the end of one row to the beginning of the next, just as your child will have to do when he begins to read.

Peg-boards are useful for practising left to right eye movement. Arrange rows of colours, different patterns, etc., for him to copy. Always work from left to right.

Rolling balls is a useful practice exercise and a way in which you can check your child's left to right eye movements. Ask him to stand about one and a half metres (five feet) away from a table, and opposite to you. Without moving his head, ask him to follow the ball rolling along the table with his eyes. Roll the ball so that his eyes move from left to right with the ball.

Tidying bookshelves is a constructive activity. Discuss book titles and arrange the books in order from left to right.

Pencil control

Introduce your child to the feeling of a crayon, using short, thick crayons. Allow a great deal of experiment with scribbling, drawing and colouring. When he feels familiar with crayons, introduce pencils and ensure correct pencil grip. He should hold the pencil above the sharpened point, between the thumb and middle finger, with index finger pressing on the pencil. This skill often takes a considerable time to establish, but is worth practising, as establishment of the correct way to hold the pencil is a most important asset for the commencement of writing and drawing. At this stage, only blank paper should be used.

Gradually introduce copying *form* in this order:

- Lines
- Circles
- Crosses
- Squares

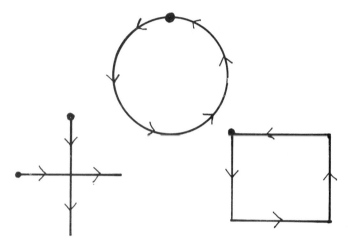

To begin with use dots to guide your child to draw pencil lines from one point to another. Then draw the line for him and ask him to draw over it as accurately as possible. Check that his direction is correct. This can be done in a variety of ways and using different colours. Progress to copying the circle shape in the same way. Here your child must use a rotary movement which moves from left to right. Complete closure of the circle is not necessary in the beginning . Practising the action is what counts. If your child is experiencing difficulty demonstrate for him and guide his hand. Practise writing in sand or in the air and only when your child feels confident to copy lines and circles, introduce crosses and rectangles in a similar way.

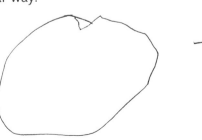

Some helpful hints

It helps to say what you are doing while you are doing it.

Examples:
When drawing a rectangle, say "Down, across to the right, up, across to the left."
When drawing a cross, say "Start here and go down, start here and go across."

Talking through an activity helps your child think in the correct sequence.

Compare things around you with the drawing of the shape.

Examples:

When practising circles, ask your child to look out for all things that are round in shape such as wheels, buttons, plates, coins, etc.
When drawing rectangles look for things that are rectangular, such as scarves, cushions, blocks, tiles, doors, etc.

Cut out the shapes which your child has drawn, or ask him to cut them out himself. Paste them into his scrapbook, cut out some similar shapes from magazines and stick them beside the shapes drawn.

When your child can successfully draw a line, practise drawing a row of lines. When he can draw a circle, practise drawing a row of circles, and similarly, when he can draw a line, a circle, a cross and a square, let him practise drawing rows using combinations of these forms. At first the forms which your child reproduces may vary in shape and size. He may also find it difficult to space equally when drawing a row. This is not significant in the early stages, and rather he should concentrate on good pencil grip, controlled movements and reasonably accurate representations of the form.

The reproduction of the above four shapes are basic to the formation of the letters of the alphabet. They are not easy to master and your child may require many opportunities to practise them. However, once mastered, using the correct direction, he has the rudiments of handwriting at his disposal.

Learning to use a pencil is a skill which is just like learning to ride a bicycle. First efforts are shaky, and constant practice is required. Confidence needs to be gained.

Your child should often practise:

- Colouring in, using colouring in books or shapes which have been cut out
- Tracing over shapes
- Drawing a line between two parallel lines, some straight and others curving, trying not to touch either side.

Visual skills	**Visual discrimination** The ability to discern similarities and differences between shapes, objects and symbols. Visual discrimination of forms and letters is a pre-requisite for reading and is a skill relevant to some areas of mathematical ability.

Visual memory The ability to remember and accurately reproduce what has been seen.

How to develop visual discrimination

Matching

Practise matching colours, shapes, sizes, lengths, designs and functions. Use toys, objects in the home, objects in local surroundings, or other available material. Encourage your child to talk about why things are the same or how they differ and discuss with him what he is doing – in this way his matching skills are considerably improved.

Example:
"A wheel is like a plate because they are both round."
"A jacket is like a jumper because they are clothes."
"A clock is like a watch because they both show us the time."

Playing cards Use a pack of playing cards. Ask your child to match colours, suits, shapes, pictures, numbers. There are a variety of games which can be played or informal exercises which can be practised using a simple pack of cards. For example, play the game 'Snap' or 'Happy Families'.

Fabric Match pieces of coloured fabrics in terms of colour, length or design.

Peg-board Use a peg-board and ask your child to match a pattern which you have created.

Size and colour At home, ask your child to match books for shape or colour; to match plates for size; or to match clothes in terms of size or colour.

Number Write a number on a piece of paper or a card and ask your child to find that number written in magazines or newspapers. Do the same using letters.

What's missing? Using magazines, pictures, or your own drawings, cover up or omit part of a picture. Ask your child to guess which part is missing. He can do similar exercises for you to guess.

Examples:
Draw a face with the eyebrows missing. Your child must show or tell you what is missing.
Draw a house with no door, a hand with no finger nails and so on.

How to develop visual memory

Visual memory — remembering what one sees is a skill which can be sharpened with practice.

Practice activities

The tray game Place a number of items on a tray. Let your child look at it, then cover the tray and ask him to remember what was on the tray. Start using two items, and slowly build up to six or seven.

Another tray game Place four or five objects on a tray. Allow your child to look for a brief period. Turn him away and remove one object then ask him to turn back and tell you what is missing.

Observation Ask your child to look out of the window, observe what he sees, turn his back to the window and describe what he has seen.

Visits Ask your child to describe visits to places such as the zoo, friends' houses or holidays, rewarding him for every item remembered.

Flash cards Make some cards with a number or letter on each, and ask your child to look at the card for five seconds. Remove the flash card and ask him to tell you what he has seen. When he correctly remembers one letter or number, try this game using cards with two letters or numbers on them, and *slowly* build up to four or five.

Patterns As described previously in this book, use pegboards and blocks for your child to copy patterns and then reproduce them from memory.

More practice

Ask your child to close his eyes and tell you what he is wearing.

As you walk, or drive in a car, or ride on a bus, ask him to predict what familiar landmarks will come up next, or what landmarks you have already passed. When the ride is over, ask him to name two or three of the landmarks passed.

If your child is interested in letters, write his name carefully on a large piece of paper. Then ask him to close his eyes and, while his eyes are closed, cover one of the letters. Ask him to look at the name again and tell you which letter is missing.

When you read to your child, ask him to discuss a picture on a previous page or, if the book is familiar, ask him to predict the picture which is coming next.

Describe a person or a place or an object with as much visual detail as possible. Ask your child to guess who or what you are describing.

Always praise or reward your child for good performance but avoid comment on failure.

Drawing people

Art is a natural, spontaneous activity for children. All children are creative and drawing, painting and modelling help your child to express his view of the world in his own way. Children do not represent things the way they look to adults. They draw and paint their own world in their own way.

An ability to draw people involves fine motor skills, hand/eye skills, and a good awareness of one's body. To understand your child's development you should be aware that there is a particular sequence in which drawing skills are typically acquired.

The scribbling age A child's earliest scribbles are random marks on paper, which later become pictures.

Disorganised scribbling At this very early stage crayons or pencils are held awkwardly, often upside down or sideways. Pencil control is not developed and movements are uncontrolled but enjoyable. Early scribbling is often done in dirt or sand, as well as on surfaces such as tables, papers and walls! Your child will have considerable difficulty keeping his scribbles on the paper or within a defined area.

Organised scribbling At some time your child discovers that there is a connection between his movements and the marks he makes. Lines begin to show vertical and circular patterns. The amount of time spent drawing increases with age, interest and ability. The child's grip on his pencil or crayon becomes more controlled. His enjoyment at this stage comes from the sensation of movement and control.

Named scribbles At this stage the child indentifies the marks he makes. While drawing, he may say "This is my dad" or "I am playing". The drawings are still very simple. Adults often think they are meaningless but, to the child they are very meaningful.

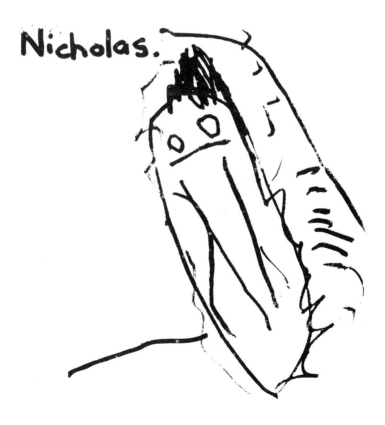

The representational stage At the beginning of this stage, the child's drawings may look unformed, but the child is carefully drawing things that have some relationship to his world. Drawings become more controlled and satisfaction comes when your child succeeds in making a recognisable drawing. Colour is often enjoyed for its own sake but may not relate to reality at this stage. A favourite subject of children is people. Children's earliest attempts at drawing people are primitive with sun-like faces. During this stage, most children's drawings of people become more sophisticated, but remain simple, with stick-like limbs often coming from the head. Gradually drawings of people emerge in proportion, with more clearly defined heads, bodies, and limbs. Very often by the end of this stage your child has developed a drawing style which he enjoys and repeats over and over again.

It is important that your child moves through *all* these phases of development. Remember that all children progress at their own rate. Those who may seem behind will usually catch up, given proper encouragement, time and, of course, opportunities.

Teaching activities for drawing people

Ask your child to look at a photograph of himself. Talk about how he looks. For example, say "Most people have two eyes and two arms" etc. Then talk about how people may differ. For example, "People have different colour hair, eyes or skin or body shape". Then ask your child to try to draw a picture of himself. When he finishes his drawing look at it with him. Have him look at himself in the mirror, or a photograph, to see if there is anything else that could be added to his picture. Pin up his drawings around the house.

Family pictures Ask your child to talk about people in his family, about the activities they enjoy doing, and about how they differ from one another. Have him draw a picture of his family doing something together. Let him tell you about his picture – what each member of the family is doing.

Silly people Fold a large piece of paper into three parts. Ask your child to draw a head and neck in the top

section. After your child has completed that fold the paper down to cover the top section and expose the middle part. Next, tell your child to draw a body and arms. After that is completed, fold the paper so that the bottom third is left. In the bottom third your child should draw legs and feet. Unfold the paper and examine the resulting picture. Discuss what is missing, or what may be added. This is an amusing activity which most children enjoy.

Faces Talk to your child about different parts of the face: eyes, nose, mouth, ears, eyelids, eyelashes, teeth, tongue, lips, beards, moustaches, hair. Draw the outline of a face for your child and have him fill in the details. The drawings may be humorous or imaginary.

Masks Talk about masks that people may wear, for example, the mask of a hero, a princess, a monster, a cowboy. Prepare a paper plate for your child by making a small hole on either side of the plate. Tie a piece of string through the hole so that the mask will fit on his head. Encourage your child to decide where the features should be and help him cut out the necessary parts, i.e., for eyes, nose and mouth. He can colour or draw the remaining area of the mask.

When your child first goes into his classroom he is sure to be bombarded with spoken instruction, comments and directions, and his language will be the way in which he will be able to communicate adequately with his teachers and his friends. If your child is unused to expressing his ideas and thoughts easily he will be at a disadvantage and may lose confidence. You can help!

Here is your check list. Before starting school your child should know:

- Names of body parts
- Personal information – name, address, etc.
- Position words – example: on, next to, behind
- Direction words – example: up, down, left, right
- Some letters by sound and name
- Colours
- How to communicate – his needs and his thoughts
- Memory words, for example, days of the week
- Some numbers

Body Parts

Why?

A child's body is what he knows first. The ability to name body parts will help him to know how his body works and will help him follow instructions which use these names. Such instructions are commonplace in a school situation. For example, teachers may instruct children to look over their shoulders to see who sits behind them, or stretch their arms and stand on their toes.

Here is a sensible list of names of body parts which your pre-school child should know:

face	trunk	limbs
mouth	neck	arms
eyes	chest	legs
ears	stomach	hands
hair	waist	fingers
nose	back	toes
chin	shoulders	thumbs
teeth	hip	wrists
tongue		ankles
eyebrows		heels
eye lashes		knees
		feet

How to teach names of body parts

Touch a part of your body, say its name, then ask your child to touch the same part of his body and name it. Reverse the roles, sometimes making deliberate mistakes to see if your child can spot them.

Draw a person on a large sheet of paper, or use a picture from a magazine or newspaper, and ask your child to show you various parts of the person's body. Award stars or stickers for correct responses.

Is it a body part? Say a series of words such as bed, chair, leg, table. Ask your child to say which is the body part or to clap when he hears its name.

Balloon hitting Ask your child to hit a balloon with various parts of his body. For example, ask him to hit the balloon with his head, or his elbow, or his knee.

Which body parts? Ask your child to close his eyes. Touch him and ask him to guess which part of the body is being touched.

What's missing? Draw a face or a body with a part missing and see if your child can guess which part it is. He must *name* the missing part not point to it.

Benefits of the knowledge of body parts

Training of the above skills will:

- Encourage a listening attitude
- Strengthen memory
- Improve observation
- Produce more mature drawing of people

Personal Information

Why?

When moving from the comfort and security of home to the larger and unfamiliar environment of school it is vital that your child knows who he is and where he belongs. By this we mean he should have a sound knowledge of:

- His name
- His age
- The name of his brothers or sisters (if any)
- The name of his city or town
- His address
- His birthday
- His parents' names

Even more important is that, in an emergency situation, your child should be able to give his name and address clearly and automatically.

Here are some ideas on how to teach these skills.

Name

Teach full name and in sequence, first, middle and last name. Let your child practise answering to his full name. For example "Will Michael John Fisher please come to the breakfast table!" "Would Michael John Fisher like marmalade on his toast?". Say your child's first name and ask him to respond with his last name, and vice versa.

Age

Ask your child to show you how old he is, using his fingers.

Show your child how old he is using birthday candles. Indicate that at his next birthday he will need one more candle. Use sweets, nuts or raisins to show your child how old he is now and how old he will be on his next birthday.

Names of brothers, sisters and parents

Find family photographs or draw a family tree. Talk to your child about the family relationships.

Ask your child to draw various members of the family and discuss how they are related to him.

Name of town or city

Pin up some pictures of your child's town or city. Comment on these pictures as often as possible, using the name of the town or the city.

Address

Point out house numbers and street names to your child.

Use your daily post to show your child the number of his house or flat.

Whilst out walking, point out different numbers on different doors.

Play postman games, delivering letters to different numbered boxes.

Practise saying your child's address and perhaps telephone number over and over again with him. Ask your child to repeat it when appropriate and possible.

Birthday

Discuss with your child the months of the year. Familiarise him with the different names. Discuss the name of the month when your child was born. Discuss other things that happen in that month, for example the type of weather to expect, whether there are holidays, what outings he may go on during that month. When your child remembers his birthday month, mention the date of his birthday. Count up to that date. Repeat as frequently as necessary.

Your child may enjoy discussing the addresses and birthdays of people close to him.

Some useful games

You could act out a situation of your child being lost and then being found, requiring him to give you his correct name and address. Telephone games are useful, for example, a telephone call to a grandparent or friend, giving details of name and address for the delivery of presents.

Benefits of sound knowledge of personal information

- Your child will come to realise the importance of remembering his teacher's name, his friends' names, his classroom number, his school address, etc.
- He should now respond when being called by name in formal situations.
- He should feel less worried about getting lost.

Position and direction words

Why?

A child is given a multitude of spoken directions during the school day. Some of these include instructions about organising himself, his work or his school possessions. These may relate to written work or general classroom behaviour, and often include some of the following words:

up/down	in/out
top/middle/bottom	over/under
open/closed	go/stop
high/low	inside/outside
beginning/end	on/off
near/far	above/below
forward/backward	toward/away
centre/corner/side	straight/crooked
through/around	coming/going
front/back	right/left
right/middle/left	to/from
here/there	in front of/behind

Understanding position and direction words

Try to be practical and see that your child *understands* the given word *before* you expect him to use it.

Examples:
Put a ball in a box and say "I am putting the ball *into* the box".
Put a cushion under the chair and say "I am putting the cushion *under* the chair".

When you feel sure that he understands the position word, ask him where the ball is, or where the cushion is, and he should be able to use the word you have demonstrated. This idea can be expanded in a great variety of ways.

Remember to show and check only one position/direction word at a time.

Right and left needs special mention Many adults and children are confused about right and left and it often takes a long time to learn these terms. Saturate your child with an awareness of right and left. To avoid confusion, use the word 'right' for some time before using the word 'left', or vice versa.

By now your child should be familiar with holding a pencil or crayon. Remind him constantly that he draws or writes with his right or left hand, whichever may be his preferred hand. Put a mark, for example, a star or a dot, on that hand for a period of time, and show that his chosen hand is the one with the dot on it.

Games are useful. Your child may be asked to throw, roll, or kick a ball with his right or left hand or leg, or touch his left ear, close his right eye, etc. Then extend the use of the word to practical situations. For example, ask him to turn left at the gate, or fetch the book on the right hand shelf, etc.

More games for position or direction words

Toys on shelves Using shelves, show your child which is the top shelf, the middle shelf, the bottom shelf. Practise

putting objects on the top, or the middle, or bottom shelves. Build on this skill by saying "put the box *under* the cat", "Put the cat *next* to the doll", "put the doll *beside* the bear".

Where is the toy? Use a container and a collection of small toys or objects. Encourage your child to play with toys and as he plays ask him to put the toys in different places. For example, "Put the doll *under* the box", or "Put the car *beside* the box", or *"inside* the box".

Sandwiches Top, middle and bottom are successfully illustrated when making sandwiches.

Picture books Find a colourful picture in a book or magazine and ask your child to tell you where several things are in the picture using position and direction words.

The bird is *in* the tree.
The leaves are *on* the branch.
The flower is *under* the tree.
The cow is *beside* the gate.
The rabbit is running *through* the grass.

Try to practise *all* the words in the position/direction words list.

The alphabet

Why?

It has been noted that "The best way to predict how well a child will read at the age of eight and a half is how many letters and letter sounds he or she knows at the age of four."* This task is not as difficult as it sounds, and the knowledge can be acquired in a most relaxed and incidental way. Here's how:

Alphabet sounds

Buy or make an alphabet frieze for your child. Show him the letter which starts his name. Emphasise the letter *sound*, rather than its name, e.g. "Let's find a 'sss' for Susan". (When the letter is written 3 times in this book, it indicates the letter *sound* not the letter name.) Then introduce four or five other letters relating to names of other family members, one at a time and over a period of weeks. Next, ask your child to find a 'sss' for Susan, or the 'juh' for Jane. Encourage him to ask other adults or older children to point out the *sound* of the first letter in their names and show it to him on his alphabet frieze.

Introduce your child to the *sound* of each of the letters in the alphabet. When he recognises five or six sounds, introduce him to the idea that 'sss' is for Susan but also for Snake and Sand. Exaggerate the 'sss' so that he *really* hears it. Ask him to think of another 'sss' word. Give him some suggestions, then move on to another sound and try to get him to think of words beginning with that sound.

This idea comes very quickly to some children and less so to others. If your child doesn't grasp the idea, continue giving him a little information about a few letters and letter sounds and try again at a later stage. It may be useful to start with the sounds which are easily seen when formed by the lips, such as 'mmm', and 'bbb'. When he has learnt to *SOUND*, not to *SAY* the alphabet, play games with an alphabet frieze or alphabet book. For example – "Show me the sound for dog". "Show me the sound which comes after 'sss'." "Show me the sound which comes before 'bbb'." Point to each letter saying its sound, and ask him to think of a word which starts with the letter *sound*, (never the letter name). All words begin with letter sounds, and knowledge of them is an essential pre-reading skill.

*Sunday Times, July 10th 1988.

Games to play

Make up funny sentences

Examples:
Funny Freddy found a frog.
Silly Sam sat on a snake.
Baby Bessie bit a bun.

Here the child must use words starting with the same sound. Point to the written letter of the sound using the frieze or an alphabet book.

I-Spy This can be played at home, or outside the home, or while driving or walking. Again, give the SOUND of the letter beginning the word.

Spot the sound While out, ask your child to look for things which begin with sounds he already knows, say, 'mmm' or 'sss'. For example, 'mmm' for motor car 'sss' for sun.

Write some letters on pieces of paper or card and, using Blu-Tack, ask your child to put the 'fff' on the fridge because 'fff' is for fridge, or the 'mmm' on the mirror because 'mmm' is for mirror, or the 'bbb' on the bath because 'bbb' is for bath, and so on.

REMEMBER THAT UP TO NOW YOU ARE STILL USING SOUNDS ONLY.

Alphabet names

When your child is beginning to be familiar with letter sounds, recognises several and associates them with words, it is time for you to tell him that letters have *names* as well as *sounds*.

You can:

- If you know it, sing the alphabet song.
- Practise saying the alphabet parrot fashion. Say the alphabet to your child, stopping occasionally to ask him to tell you the next letter or letters.
- Say the alphabet, one letter at a time and ask your child to say the corresponding sound.

- Write individual letters on pieces of paper and ask your child to match the letter on his frieze, in his books or magazines, etc.
- Buy alphabet noodles or biscuits, and practise naming and matching letters.
- If you have a tape recorder, make a tape of your child reciting or singing the alphabet. He can practise saying the alphabet in different ways, in a high or low voice, at a fast or slow speed, quietly or loudly, in a happy, sad, or angry voice. It is always fun for children to hear themselves on tape. It also makes it easier to notice mistakes.
- Let your child recite the alphabet to appreciative audiences. A special telephone call to grandparents, a

favourite aunt or friend can really make him feel important when learning this new skill.

Reminders

Introduce the *name* of a letter only when your child knows the sound of that letter.

In word/sound games, take care to suggest only words that begin with single letter sounds. Example: 'sss' for slipper and *not* 'sh' for shoes, nor 'th' for think.

Some children enjoy sound games, others don't. Never continue these games if your child is not interested

If they appeal, sound games may be extended in many ways.

Examples:

Picking out sounds in signs
Picking out sounds in magazines and newspapers
Playing 'I-Spy' whilst walking, driving or bathing
Playing sounding games such as 'ggg' for gate, 'hhh' for house, 'sss' for soap, ad nauseam!

Immerse your child in sounds!

Benefits of good knowledge of sound

- When your child knows letter sounds, he has a built-in reading kit. The next logical step leads to word building, which is putting the sounds together to form words, e.g. c-a-t = cat. This is READING.

- Good knowledge of sounds makes for good spelling
- Memory, observation, and attention are sharpened
- Poor knowledge of sounds makes for delayed reading ability.

Colours

Why?

We live in a world of colour, an awareness of which helps us to make choices, use information, and adds to the richness of what we see.

How to teach colour

Match colours Use beads, blocks, pencils, clothes, books, fabric, etc., for playing matching games.

When your child can consistently match colours, encourage him to repeat after you the colour name, and then to progress to naming colours on his own. Make sure he learns only one colour at a time.

Some useful activities

Scrapbook Make a scrapbook of colours.

Colour 'searches' For example "Find me a blue jumper," etc.

Talk about the colours of flowers, etc.

Have a 'Colour day'

Example:
On a chosen day wear something yellow, have yellow food, colour a yellow picture, tie a yellow thread around the child's finger, thread yellow beads, put a yellow sticker or spot on all things that are yellow.

Pictures Look at pictures and pick out different colours.

Benefits of colour knowledge

- It encourages greater appreciation of surroundings
- It gives the ability to sort and choose by colour
- Colour knowledge helps a child recognise the colour-coded signals in the world around him
- It encourages improved ability to describe what he sees

Talking and conversation

Why?

One of the most valuable things you can do for your child is to talk to him. Easier said than done. Parents are mostly busy, often tired, and tempted to encourage their children to watch television. There is much evidence to suggest that television programmes can be of benefit to your child, but talking is more important. Don't let television become the "plug-in drug". Conversation can do so much for your child's development. Talk, talk and more talk is a rewarding diet.

How to encourage talking and conversation

Widen your child's experience

Try to take your child out of his daily environment at least once a month. Useful places to visit which provide much opportunity for new language experience are zoos, fun parks, children's museums, sightseeing trips, a day in the country or city, a visit to the seaside. When choosing a

place of interest, talk to your child about it before going. Possibly show him pictures of the place, discuss what he will see and what he may expect. If you can, answer the questions which inevitably arise.

On arriving at your destination, try to collect postcards, souvenirs or take photographs, or collect objects such as leaves or shells, which may help your child remember the experience.

When you get home, use a scrap-book to remind him of what he has seen and done.

Encourage him to remember his outing, to tell others about it and to add his own ideas for his scrap-book. Use the opportunity to widen your child's vocabulary – introduce new words, but only those which relate to that day's events.

Reading to your child

Five-year-olds who have been read to have better speech and language ability than those who have not had this experience. Giving children successful and enjoyable experiences with books creates the desire to read.

Try to read to your child several times a week. We are always told to choose appropriate books but, in the beginning, whatever your child likes is right. When he becomes used to listening to stories, begin to include books which *you* think would be interesting and enjoyable. Too often, a child enjoys the reading experience only because it allows him a quiet five minutes of the sole attention of the parent in a cosy, loving situation. He becomes lulled by the sound of your voice and your closeness. If you stop to discuss the story, you may find that he hasn't listened to a word of it or has become sleepy.

Remedy

When reading to your child, it is essential to:

● Stop after a brief introduction to the story, discuss the story so far, the people in it and what may or may not happen next. If your child shows no interest; or is tired, the chances are that the book or the time may not be suitable. Try another book or another time as

often as you need until he shows some real interest. Start on simple books first – any reading experience is a valuable one.

- Introduce new words from the story by talking about them and possibly showing the child the real thing or a picture of the real thing. Use these new words in conversation as often as possible so that they become part of his vocabulary.
- Ask your child to try and retell the story by looking at the pictures.
- Re-read stories, asking your child to fill in a missing word, or end a sentence. Example: Jack climbed … (…the beanstalk). Frequently discuss stories you have read to him.
- Allow your child to handle the book and become aware of turning pages one at a time. Reading should be a 'hands on' experience.

As a guideline for parents, it may be helpful to know that children between the ages of four and seven typically develop reading skills in the following sequences.*

A child:

- Turns book right side up
- Turns pages several at a time
- Points to and names simple pictures
- Wants to hear a story repeated
- Takes part in reading by saying words and phrases
- Recites a familiar book in an attempt to 'read' from memory
- Attempts to 'read' by looking at the illustrations
- Starts reading some words by sight
- Begins to sound out the letters of simple words
- Begins to blend the sounds to make a word
- Reads simple words, some by recognition, others by sounding and blending

Spend as much time on each stage as is necessary.

Other suggestions

Join a local library.

Your child should listen to children's radio programmes which tell stories.

*Albert H. Brigance, *Reading Readiness: Strategies and Practice*, (Massachusetts, Curriculum Associates, 1985).

Possibly buy story cassettes. They can become favourites, provided they are supplemented by discussion and comment by you as your part of the talk, talk, talk programme. But also let your children talk. Talkative parents often have silent children.

Invent stories with your child.

Look through the book before reading it to your child. Reading aloud comes naturally to very few people and requires preparation to allow you to plan the expression to use for a passage, to decide which text to shorten, eliminate or elaborate.

Select short books. When first presenting books to a child, select picture books with only a few pages, because the attention span of the child will probably be short. The book that can be read quickly is best. Select books with large pictures that do not include a lot of detail.

Select books with simple story lines and repetition. If the story is repetitive, a child will usually participate in reading it.

Select books about subjects that you know interest your child. Many children enjoy wordless books which present a plot through illustrations.

Children relate best to pictures and photographs of events, people and places within their own experience, rather than pictures about fantasies. They tend to respond enthusiastically to pictures of animals.

If a child asks, re-read a book. Frequently he will want a favourite story read time after time. Vary the story each time by asking different questions, by letting the child tell you what is going to happen next and by talking about the pictures and letting your child act out parts of the story.

Plan a suitable seating arrangement so that your child can see the illustrations as you read the book. When he begins to develop reading readiness skills, have him sit so that he can see the words. Point to the words as you read them to train his left to right eye movement.

In the beginning plan short story times (possibly only five minutes) and, as your child's attention span increases, introduce longer story times. To avoid behaviour problems and a dislike of stories, it is important that the time devoted to story reading is not longer than his attention span.

Have several books available. Always allow your child to choose the story he wants.

Teach your child to take care of books. Encourage him to discuss ways he can take care of books, for example,

- He should have clean hands when looking at a book
- It is better for him not to eat while looking at a book
- He should be sure a surface is clean before placing a book on it
- It is sensible to carry books in a plastic bag and to keep them from getting dirty or wet
- Discuss and demonstrate how turning pages from the top prevents bent and torn pages
- Talk about what can happen to a book if it is left outside or left where pets can get at it.

Vocabulary

Follow your child's lead and try to give him the names of the things he asks about. Some of these, together with the words he has met through all the suggested activities, can be stored in a picture scrap-book by either sticking in a picture about the word or drawing what the word represents. From time to time look back through this store of words. Revise them by using them when chatting.

| **Memory words** | There are certain words that your child should know from memory: These are: |

- Days of the week
- Months of the year
- Counting to ten or more

Memory words must first be heard, so therefore *tell* your child these sequences frequently. Let him say them with you, on his own, or with other children.

Days of the week

Often recite the days of the week in order. Remind your child which day it is. Discuss which day comes next. Discuss which day comes after that.

Discuss special days, birthdays, Christmas, family outings etc., naming the day on which they fall.

Examples:
"On Tuesday it will be your birthday."
"On Wednesday we are going to see Granny."

Months of the year

Some general introduction to the months of the year is useful, but a young child is not expected to remember them all in correct sequence. Discuss the month of your child's birthday, the month of Christmas, Easter and also the seasons of the year. Children often like to know when other people's birthdays fall. Buy a Birthday Book for him to put in favourite people's birthdays. Let him draw his own interpretations of the seasons of the year

Word counting

Give your child much repetition of the numbers 1 to 10 in frequent short spells and let him count objects around him.

Use rhymes and songs and finger play.

Example: 'One, Two, Buckle My Shoe,' 'This Old Man'. Here is a favourite from 'Mother Goose'.

One, two, buckle my shoe,
Three, four, knock at the door,
Five, six, pick up sticks,
Seven, eight, lay them straight,
Nine, ten, a good fat hen.

Count steps, paving stones, lamp-posts, candles on a cake, shoes and whatever happens to come your way.
Perhaps you could make up some counting rhymes of your own.

Some word and memory games

Grouping objects

Ask your child to name some . . .

colours
animals
birds
flowers

To begin with, start the game by giving him two or three suggestions.

"Tell me some things that are . . ."

heavy
hot
soft
rough
high

"Tell me how a ----- and a ---- are alike."

cat/dog
lorry/car
house/tent
snow/salt
helicopter/aeroplane
carrot/potato
skirt/shoe
letters/book
daffodil/dandelion

"Say words that go together"

ladies and ---
fathers and ---
sisters and ---
kings and ---
uncles and ---

Your child should guess the missing word.

Odd one out Ask your child which doesn't belong:

cat, dog, lorry, pig, mouse.
Peter, John, David, Susan.
fat, green, blue, red, white.

Opposites Again, ask your child to guess the missing word:

This hand is clean, but that one is -----.
This lift is going up, but that one is coming -----.
He is my father, she is my ------.
This pencil is long, but that one is ----.

Repetition – words and sentences. Train your child to remember a list of short words. Start with three and increase as his ability increases. Let him make some up for you too. If you feel he is ready, see if he can remember some simple sentences. For example, play "I went to the shops and bought a ball." "I went to the shops and bought a ball and a bat." and so on.

Following directions This is a very important skill to develop in readiness for school and it should be encouraged in a variety of ways.

Put six or seven objects in front of your child (for instance, coloured pencils, boxes, fruit) and give him directions which gradually get longer, such as:

Put the red pencil in the box.
Put the red and green pencils in the box.
Put the red pencil in the biggest box.
Put the red pencil in the smallest box and then give me an
   apple.

| **Stimulating imagination** | Using your imagination is an important asset which will assist your child in future creative writing, i.e., the ability to express his ideas and feelings easily on paper. Young children have far greater ability and desire to write stories than is generally expected. |

Ask your child to imagine himself doing a job, for example, "Imagine you are a doctor. What would you use, and what would you do?"

Ask your child to think of all the things that he might see in a supermarket, see on the beach, see in the park, etc. Discuss some situations, such as:

What would he do if he saw a house on fire?
What would he do if his dog was lost?

Some examples of early creative writing in school.

General helpful hints

Give your child a chance. Don't always anticipate what he has to say. Remember, talking is a new skill for him and it may take him some time to get his thoughts across. Give him lots of time and your attention. In the same way, if he were learning to ride a bicycle you would not expect him to pedal away without help.

Think of conversation as a game of table tennis. It is a question of give and take. Don't hog the ball. Take turns. Keep the ball moving. The more turns he has, the more practice for him.

Try to make story-telling interesting for your child, reading with animation and enthusiasm. If you are not sure what your child wishes to say, ask him appropriate questions to help him feel that he is communicating with you and what he needs to say is important.

Find occasions to ask his opinion about events and happenings.

Too many orders and commands are conversation stoppers.

Benefits of talking and conversation

Talking and conversation = communication and this in turn:

- Builds confidence
- Helps your child approach his new teacher, other children and adults in his environment with ease
- Gives your child the ability to express himself
- Helps him understand instructions better
- Makes early learning situations a source of enjoyment
- Leads to wider vocabulary which, in turn, creates a better reader

Number

Why?

Basic knowledge of number comes into everyday life and is a skill needed from the start.

How to teach number

When your child can recognise and recite the numbers from 1 to 10 introduce a lively number frieze to him, that is, the numbers 1 to 10 in a row with the correct corresponding number of dots, stars or pictures beneath or beside the figure.

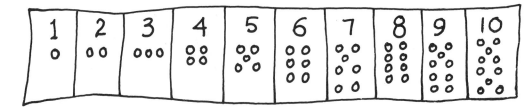

Then, beginning with only the numbers 1 and 2, show him how many each represents, and that they are *different* amounts . Lots of practice, using raisins, books, shoes, toys, dots, anything at all is needed to teach your child the value of 1 or the value of 2.

Only when your child understands how many 1 and 2 are, introduce the number 3. Spend at least a week asking your child to select 3 stones, 3 biscuits, 3 toys, etc., as frequently as possible during the day. When 3 is established, go on to number 4, and so on. Spend as much time as you can, establishing the name and *value* of each number. As often as possible, ask your child to give you, say, 1 biscuit, or 2 cherries, 3 potatoes, or whatever is at hand.

If your child is accustomed to using a crayon or a pencil, ask him to trace over large numbers which you have written, and let him draw the number of dots required for each number.

To help your child recognise the look of a number, point it out to him on buses, on his frieze, on houses, on doors, on clocks and on pages.

Remember – lots of praise.

Number activities and games

Recognition Write the numbers 1 to 10 on paper and ask your child to circle or mark the number you call out.

Sorting Let your child sort beans, marbles, raisins into twos, threes, fours, etc.

Number badges Stick or pin a paper number on your child. It is his number for the day. Match it with other numbers, eat that many raisins, draw it, etc.

Tasks Ask your child to fetch a particular number of objects. Reward him for correct results.

Benefits of a good number sense

Number sense enables a child to:

- Calculate
- Make judgements
- Think logically
- Cope with the beginning of formal mathematics

Quantity words

Apart from actual numbers, it will be of great benefit to your child to know *quantity words*. Suggestions for quantity words to be taught and materials that can be used for teaching the meaning of the words are as follows:

little/big: boards, boxes, rocks, buttons, articles of clothing; all of different sizes.

short/long: strips of paper, pencils, string, rope, straws, sticks. Ensure that there is a clear difference in the lengths.

some/none: empty containers, containers filled with stones, marbles, beads, popcorn.

thin/fat: strips of paper, thin and fat articles made from plasticine, pencils, etc.

few/many: boxes or other containers filled with stones, shells, marbles, nuts, raisins.

thick/thin: pieces of wood, cloth, cardboard; all of different thicknesses.

light/heavy: pieces of wood, pebbles, metal; all of different weights.

narrow/wide: pieces of wood, strips of cloth, strips of paper cut into different widths.

shallow/deep: drinking glasses, pans, pots, bowls to be filled or semi-filled with water.

small/medium: golf balls, tennis balls, stones, fruit, buttons, articles of clothing, all different sizes.

half/whole: sandwiches, sheets of paper, paper plates, fruit.

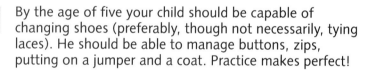

Why?

When your child first starts school, there will be some new and different social demands to be met. Apart from the academic value of education, we must remember it also develops good social behaviour and friendships essential in life, and provides the opportunity for learning self-control and self-help skills. These in turn will give your child self-reliance and therefore self-esteem.

The social skills necessary for school include:

- Independence in dressing, eating and toiletting
- Sharing
- Respecting property at school and at home
- Learning to take turns
- Learning about lending and borrowing
- Organisational skills

Dressing

By the age of five your child should be capable of changing shoes (preferably, though not necessarily, tying laces). He should be able to manage buttons, zips, putting on a jumper and a coat. Practice makes perfect!

How to teach dressing

First teach your child to dress a large toy.

Allow enough time before going out for your child to try to dress himself. Remember that many children have difficulties in dressing and need time to practise.

Choose clothes that are easy to put on.

Set out clothes in correct sequence, to help speed the process. Try to help your child to recognise the front and back of his clothes by showing him labels etc.

Say out aloud each step as he dresses. For example, "and next you put on your socks." Pause. "Now, your shoes." Ask him to say what he is doing as he dresses. This is an extra aid to help him concentrate on his dressing, avoid distraction and speed up the process.

Use clothing from the laundry basket for him to practise buttons, fasteners and zips.

Have a box of old clothes with different fastenings. Play dressing-up games with these.

Have different coloured dots on feet and matching dots on shoes for your child to match shoe and foot.

If your child shows interest in tying bows, it helps to

learn using laces in two colours. Laces can be hung up, e.g., on a door knob, for practice.

Helpful suggestions

Eating

Set aside adequate time for meals, making it clear to your child that he must wait for the meal to end before leaving the table, as will be expected of him at school. It helps to keep his interest going by making a few meals a week happy social occasions in which he plays an important part. For example, ask him to select his favourite foods, or help lay the table. Present something unusual, such as pink food, or a funny-face pudding – anything to keep his attention and the conversation going. Side-track the impulsive table-leaver by keeping a surprise for the end, by discussing his day, or planning his tomorrow while the meal is in progress.
Encourage correct use of cutlery by giving him many opportunities to practise with a spoon and fork. Later, practise cutting on a slice of bread or soft vegetables and fruit.

Tea parties, or an outing for tea are helpful to accustom your child to eating with people outside the family group.

Imaginary games, using (if you can bear it) real utensils for eating, are also good practice opportunities.

Encourage your child to be more experimental with food. Outside the home, he is bound to be offered food

he has not tasted before – he needs to know how to respond.

| Toiletting |

Helpful suggestions

Independent proper use of the lavatory is vital. Remember, at school, your child will have to share the use of the lavatory with many other children, so . . .

Teach the difference between sufficient and excessive use of lavatory paper.

Flushing the lavatory after use should be a habit, but often is a habit neglected. This *must* be established before coming to school. Just think of it – multiply a slack, flushing habit of one child by that of two to five hundred others! It helps if you familiarise your child with different flushings. Many children actually find the subject quite fascinating. Reward good flushers!

Discuss the importance of washing hands after using the lavatory. Establish the habit by reminders and checks.

Sharing

A young child often does not understand about sharing, and *you* need to help him. Your child will have to share books, equipment, toys, teacher's time, etc., and if he is a 'hogger', he is sure to suffer and may become unpopular.

Helpful suggestions

Buy a bar of chocolate to be shared, instead of one for each person.

Allow him to share some of your possessions, such as your scarf, or pencils, or hair brushes, etc.

Encourage him to share his toys or books with others in the house, or with friends.

Share television and radio time. Make sure he knows *you* have a right to the television set, video or cassette player.

He must learn to share the attention of the adult in charge, and not expect always to be centre stage. Occasionally, introduce a waiting period before agreeing to a request, but do remember to keep your side of the bargain.

Example:
If a child wants a story read at an inconvenient time for you, firmly but gently say that you will read it, for example, after tea. He is learning to await his turn. This is an *essential* classroom skill.

Respecting property at school and at home

This skill starts with your child respecting his *own possessions.* He has to learn to treat books and toys with care, and to put them away after use. These good habits will strengthen his independence and prove invaluable for him at school.

Helpful suggestions

Make a joint effort. Choose a time when you are not at your wits' end, or in the middle of preparing dinner, and share the tidying tasks. Give fulsome praise for efforts made.

If there is more than one child in the family, the children could take turns to put away and tidy the toys. A roster system with rewards may be useful.

Always explain the need to keep all parts of the game or puzzle together. Discuss the 'serious issue' of missing parts, and how the game cannot be used again if a part is lost.

It helps if your child has a proper place in which to keep his toys and books – easily accessible to him.

A few of his very own possessions, and a place in which to keep them, go a long way to fostering a pride of ownership and a respect for the belongings of others.

Learning to take turns

'Me first' is anti-social behaviour, and can prove to be a child's own worst enemy in group situations. Expose your child to a multitude of special situations in which he will *have* to be second, third, or even last, without feeling second best. The earlier you begin, the easier it will be.

Encourage your child wherever possible to:

- Take turns to choose: what to eat, what to play, which story to read, who baths first, etc.
- Take turns to tell funny stories
- Take turns with building blocks, or using colours
- Take turns to keep the penny change
- Take turns to keep the bus tickets

Lending and borrowing

Helpful suggestions

Outings to the library are very valuable lessons in borrowing and returning, and are also an excellent introduction to a library and its uses.

Be sure that anything your child borrows is returned. It is important that he understands the difference between a gift and a loan.

To teach your child the idea of lending, purposely borrow something of his, but be sure to return the borrowed item or the lesson will be lost!

Many children find it difficult to loosen their grip on their possessions, so begin with asking to borrow something which you know your child will easily give up. Progress then to more treasured possessions.

Planning and organisational skills

When your child starts school perhaps for the first time in his life he will have to be responsible for his possessions and ready to respond to group organisation. This need not prove a problem if he has begun to learn the idea of *preparation*.

Helpful suggestions

Use his knowledge of the days of the week. List activities and say what is needed for them.

Examples:
"Today we are going swimming. Let's get our swimming things ready."
"Tomorrow we are going to visit Grandma. Let's get everything ready to take."

Extend the planning with, say, drawing the actions in the right order, or drawing the sequence of events to take place . Either child or parent may want to draw.

Practise packing bags for spending a night away from home. Discuss what is really needed well in advance. Have dummy runs.

Play imaginary games involving preparation for going on holiday or a picnic, etc.

Play games which involve your child in knowing a *sequence* of events.

Example: Discuss the making of a pot of tea.

1 Fill the kettle with water
2 Switch on the heat
3 Warm the teapot
4 Put the tea in the teapot
5 Pour boiling water into the teapot
6 Tea is ready to serve

Ask him to describe how he would do it. This can be fun if you make a joke of any part the child omits. Other suggestions for practising sequencing are asking him how he would: post a letter, get ready for school, get ready for bed, plant a flower.

Learning to organise will help your child settle quickly and happily into school, especially if you continue to help him with planning his days during the first few weeks there. Very soon you will find that your child will be confident enough to be telling *you* what he needs for each day! Some children take naturally to organisation, others don't and need help.

Some useful hints

Make a wall chart showing the daily programme – use pictures, drawings or cut-outs of the activities and what may be needed for them.

Hang a large bag on the back of the bedroom door. In the evening ask your child to put all that is needed for the following day, e.g. pencils, gym shoes, books, etc. in the bag. This prevents the anxieties often experienced by parent and child before leaving for school, and ensures that he starts the day calmly and in good spirits.

If possible, make a separate place in the house for all school possessions.

A last thought

In this book we have tried to offer various ideas which may be helpful in preparing your child for school. Parents should not be disappointed that their efforts do not result in immediate changes and success because all these tasks require practice — little and often — before they are established.

If your child starts his schooling without anxieties and with the idea that manners *can* be fun, he will make a good first impression on his teachers and companions. GIVE YOUR CHILD THE *RIGHT START!*